Make Believe

by Kristin Anna Froberg

A Samuel French Acting Edition

FOUNDED 1830
NEW YORK HOLLYWOOD LONDON TORONTO
SAMUELFRENCH.COM

Copyright © 2009 by Kristin Anna Froberg
Cover Image by Simone Finney

ALL RIGHTS RESERVED

CAUTION: Professionals and amateurs are hereby warned that *MAKE BELIEVE* is subject to a Licensing Fee. It is fully protected under the copyright laws of the United States of America, the British Commonwealth, including Canada, and all other countries of the Copyright Union. All rights, including professional, amateur, motion picture, recitation, lecturing, public reading, radio broadcasting, television and the rights of translation into foreign languages are strictly reserved. In its present form the play is dedicated to the reading public only.

The amateur live stage performance rights to *MAKE BELIEVE* are controlled exclusively by Samuel French, Inc., and licensing arrangements and performance licenses must be secured well in advance of presentation. PLEASE NOTE that amateur Licensing Fees are set upon application in accordance with your producing circumstances. When applying for a licensing quotation and a performance license please give us the number of performances intended, dates of production, your seating capacity and admission fee. Licensing Fees are payable one week before the opening performance of the play to Samuel French, Inc., at 45 W. 25th Street, New York, NY 10010.

Licensing Fee of the required amount must be paid whether the play is presented for charity or gain and whether or not admission is charged.

Stock licensing fees quoted upon application to Samuel French, Inc.

For all other rights than those stipulated above, apply to Samuel French, Inc., at 45 W. 25th Street, New York, NY 10010.

Particular emphasis is laid on the question of amateur or professional readings, permission and terms for which must be secured in writing from Samuel French, Inc.

Copying from this book in whole or in part is strictly forbidden by law, and the right of performance is not transferable.

Whenever the play is produced the following notice must appear on all programs, printing and advertising for the play: "Produced by special arrangement with Samuel French, Inc."

Due authorship credit must be given on all programs, printing and advertising for the play.

ISBN 978-0-573-69685-5   Printed in U.S.A.   #29098

No one shall commit or authorize any act or omission by which the copyright of, or the right to copyright, this play may be impaired.

No one shall make any changes in this play for the purpose of production.

Publication of this play does not imply availability for performance. Both amateurs and professionals considering a production are strongly advised in their own interests to apply to Samuel French, Inc., for written permission before starting rehearsals, advertising, or booking a theatre.

No part of this book may be reproduced, stored in a retrieval system, or transmitted in any form, by any means, now known or yet to be invented, including mechanical, electronic, photocopying, recording, videotaping, or otherwise, without the prior written permission of the publisher.

IMPORTANT BILLING AND CREDIT REQUIREMENTS

All producers of *MAKE BELIEVE* *must* give credit to the Author of the Play in all programs distributed in connection with performances of the Play, and in all instances in which the title of the Play appears for the purposes of advertising, publicizing or otherwise exploiting the Play and/or a production. The name of the Author *must* appear on a separate line on which no other name appears, immediately following the title and *must* appear in size of type not less than fifty percent of the size of the title type.

MAKE BELIEVE had its world premiere at Salomon Theatre in San Diego on January 30, 2007. The production was directed by Paul R. Bassett. Jennifer Bantelman was the dramaturg. Jessica Bird designed the costumes, Walter Williams designed the set, and Paul R. Bassett designed the lighting. The cast was as follows:

NATASHA	Holly I. Wilson
LENA	Rebecca Duckworth
LYDIA	Katie Dupont
MIKE	Zach Hodgson
MARCUS	Phillip Moyer
LT. HARRIS	Mark Burton

MAKE BELIEVE had its New York Premiere at Manhattan Repertory Theatre on August 27, 2008. The production was directed by Elizabeth Reed. The cast was as follows:

NATASHA	Ashley Diane Currie
LENA	Caitlin Gold
LYDIA	Laura Campbell
MIKE	Jesse Sells
MARCUS	Scott Witebsky
LT. HARRIS	Alexis Savino

CHARACTERS

NATASHA
LENA
LYDIA
MIKE
MARCUS
LT. HARRIS

ACT ONE

Scene One

(NATASHA's room, evening. NATASHA LISENKO, 22, sits in front of her computer with her parents, LYDIA and MIKE, on either side. LENA, 17, stands away from the other three. NATASHA and LENA both wear one slender silver bracelet. NATASHA is wearing headphones. LENA addresses the audience; the other three don't hear her.)

LENA. They said it would be an adventure. Exclamation point. The kind of thing grown-ups always say when there's something coming and they know you won't like it.

NATASHA. You're hovering. What is it?

LYDIA. Your father and I, we've been talking –

MIKE. Thinking.

LYDIA. Praying.

NATASHA. You have not.

MIKE. And the thing is, Sport – We're just not sure the "distance learning" is working.

LENA. It's a really dirty trick if you think about it; it's like covering raisins in chocolate. It doesn't make them candy, no matter what anybody says. And it's not fair, because children are stupid – most children are stupid. My sister, Tasha, doesn't count. Somebody had to be the smart one. It wasn't going to be me.

NATASHA. I'm confused by what you mean when you say "not working." I'm learning. From a distance. That was the agreement.

LYDIA. For a *time*, Natasha. It's time to try something different.

MIKE. Take a look at what came in the mail today, Sport! Yale! Go Bulldogs! Grrr!

NATASHA. Dad, I don't care what you say. I don't care if it builds character. I will never be a mascot. Not ever.

MIKE. Of course not, of course not – not for everybody – it's a matter of preference –

LYDIA. But wouldn't it be exciting to take a trip? We could visit the campus, we could visit – lots of campuses, really – visit New York while we're there – there's Columbia, NYU – I think it would be exciting –

LENA. Exciting is another really good one. I bought it. Every time. They said it would be exciting to move to a new house and a new school and a new city, because I was six. Nobody knows when they're six. And you almost wish your sister wasn't a cracked genius who figured out how to eavesdrop without getting caught and found out what "separation" and "custody" meant before she was supposed to. Smart people have this annoying way of telling you all kinds of things it turns out you don't want to know.

NATASHA. You mean exciting for you. I don't think it's exciting.

LYDIA. Are you kidding? It's the most exciting city in the world –

NATASHA. It smells like urine.

LYDIA. How would you know, you've never been.

NATASHA. I don't need to go there to know that it smells like urine –

MIKE. Well, Natasha, any city has its problems – there are lots of similar problems right here in the Bay Area –

NATASHA. Right, so why do I need to go to the other side of the country to have problems with a city when I can have the same problems here for free –

LYDIA. "Free."

NATASHA. Mom?

LYDIA. Come to think of it you aren't paying rent, are you?

LENA. Some things, you can't swallow at that age, or at any age. Like, "Mom isn't coming." Because it's sharp and it sticks in your throat. Lucky I had Tasha to explain things to me. Even if she's not always the smart one. Even if she does dumb things, too, sometimes. Even if one time she ate an entire box of crayons to see if they tasted like what they were called.

LYDIA. New arrangement, Natasha, as of right now –

MIKE. Lydia –

LYDIA. Let me finish. We've talked about this. We've tried to give you space to – whatever you said you needed to do – "find yourself" –

NATASHA. I never said I needed to find myself.

LYDIA. But as far as I can tell all you're doing is blogging –

NATASHA. I'm not –

MIKE. You can only take so many classes online.

LYDIA. You're taking the SAT. You're getting a head start on applications for the fall semester, because you're twenty-six, Natasha, and –

NATASHA. I'm twenty-two.

LYDIA. Of course you are. I was just visualizing. I'm going to take a valium now.

(**LYDIA** *exits.* **MIKE** *lingers.*)

MIKE. The thing is, Sport – We're thinking about selling the house.

NATASHA. What?

MIKE. Just thinking. And talking.

NATASHA. It's her idea.

MIKE. No. It's something we've both been thinking about, for a while –

NATASHA. For how long?

MIKE. A while. What do you think?

NATASHA. Does it matter what I think?

MIKE. Of course. And it matters where you go to school, too, if you decide that's something you want to do –

NATASHA. It's not.

MIKE. It would affect where we move, if we move –

NATASHA. But your job – both of your jobs –

MIKE. I've been thinking about retiring.

NATASHA. What about Mom?

MIKE. These are just things we're thinking about. I know a four-year university isn't for everybody – we just don't want to see you in a rut.

NATASHA. I'm not in a rut. I'm kind of tired, dad –

MIKE. Of course. Do you want your door open or closed?

NATASHA. I don't know, Dad, it's a tough one. But considering I have a reputation as a disaffected youth to uphold –

MIKE. Good night.

NATASHA. Good night, Dad.

LENA. Good night, Dad.

(MIKE exits. NATASHA returns to her computer. LENA creeps behind her. This, NATASHA can hear.)

LENA. Hand prints. Finger prints. Crayon, on the walls. Remember how it looked when we got back? You leave your house for one year and some snotty, dirty kids mess up everything. They'd do the same thing, you know, if you left again – different people but the same mess, they'd mess up our house and our walls –

NATASHA. They wouldn't be our walls anymore. It wouldn't be our house.

LENA. So? Maybe you do want to move, get out, get away, get on a plane and go all the way to the other side of the country? Think about it, Tasha. You could ride in a tin can, way high up in the sky with all kinds of people you don't even know – all of you in the air, together, with everyone's breath and everyone's smell in everybody else's mouth and nose – wouldn't that be an 'adventure.' Wouldn't that be *exciting*?

(NATASHA turns away from LENA, back to her computer. LENA addresses the audience again.)

LENA. The day we leave for a year – a whole year, at least – she doesn't even look at the city. I know she's crying but I can't prove it because she won't put down her She-Ra Viewmaster. And traffic is so bad we can't even play our game. You have to hold your breath. On bridges, in tunnels. You have to, or else something bad will happen. Except on moving day, there's a bus crash in front of us, and we don't move for an hour and a half. Tasha plays the game better than anybody, and even she can't hold her breath that long.

Scene Two

(**NATASHA** *is in the living room, reading a magazine. There's a knock at the door. She opens it to reveal* **MARCUS**, *mid-20s.*)

MARCUS. Hi.

NATASHA. Hello.

MARCUS. Are you Natasha?

NATASHA. Are you from the Church of Jesus Christ of Latter Day Saints?

MARCUS. …No.

NATASHA. Are you sure?

MARCUS. Yes.

NATASHA. You don't seem sure.

MARCUS. I'm from Excel Tutors –

NATASHA. Okay…

MARCUS. I'm supposed to help you with the SAT –

NATASHA. Oh, you're serious. Okay. So were they. Um, come in. …this is unfortunate –

MARCUS. Why is it unfortunate?

NATASHA. There's been a misunderstanding.

MARCUS. What kind of misunderstanding?

NATASHA. You don't need to be here. It was a mix-up.

MARCUS. Oh.

NATASHA. Yeah.

MARCUS. So you're not taking the SAT.

NATASHA. No.

MARCUS. Okay. So why did – who was it, your mother –

NATASHA. Yes, I'm sure it was – um – that's more of a question for her. And she's not here right now, so you have the afternoon off! Good times. Right? You're not leaving.

MARCUS. Well, she said you'd probably say something like that –

NATASHA. Oh? Listen, Marcus, I'm sure you're busy, you have other places to be, things to do – I'm not taking the SAT. She just thinks I'm taking the SAT.

MARCUS. Why does she think that?

NATASHA. I don't know. Why does anyone think anything? Why do kids believe in Santa? These are questions for my mother, who isn't here –

MARCUS. She said you've been out of school for four years.

NATASHA. She gave you all kinds of trivia, didn't she?

MARCUS. Why are you doing this now?

NATASHA. What?

MARCUS. Why did you wait four years? I'm just curious.

NATASHA. See when you ask it like that, it makes it sound like I woke up, yesterday morning or something, and thought, "It's time. It's finally here." I promise I didn't. It's my parent's deal, their wishful thinking. I'm not really a school kind of person.

MARCUS. See, you think that –

NATASHA. No, I know that – Look, I can tell you're really fired up about education and all, I mean you must be, otherwise you'd work at Starbucks and you'd get a lot better benefits – I just – God. People like you make me really uncomfortable –

MARCUS. Uncomfortable how?

NATASHA. After-School Special uncomfortable.

MARCUS. Like Helen Hunt smoking crack and falling out a window uncomfortable?

NATASHA. No – although that is totally the best one –

*(**MARCUS** sits down and starts opening books.)*

NATASHA. Have a seat.

MARCUS. You got good grades.

NATASHA. I'm sorry?

MARCUS. In high school.

NATASHA. How do you know?

MARCUS. Your moth –

NATASHA. My mother. Right. Really helpful. Just because I got good grades doesn't mean I was interested. I wasn't.

MARCUS. So we'll start here, then.

NATASHA. What kind of idiot math is this?

MARCUS. It's just a review, just to start –

NATASHA. A Boat-In-River problem? No. Pick something else. I'm not doing that.

MARCUS. No.

NATASHA. Excuse me?

MARCUS. I think you should start here. I think this would be a good starting place.

NATASHA. I think you're on crack. This is silly, and it's pointless, and it doesn't qualify as a problem. Global Warming qualifies as a problem –

MARCUS. But this is how we're going to fix –

NATASHA. What?

MARCUS. I mean –

NATASHA. Finish the thought. You were about to tell me this problem, right here, is going to fix Global Warming.

MARCUS. Well – what I mean is, with a foundation of basic tools, it's then possible to –

NATASHA. This problem is going to fix Global Warming? I'd better take a look at it. We can't waste any time. "Craig" – that's kind of generic – we should probably call him Fitzwilliam, just to be safe – "Is in a motorboat traveling two meters per second" – there's part of his problem.

MARCUS. What?

NATASHA. He needs to pimp his ride. Now, assuming he doesn't – which he won't because he's driving a boat in the first place – he encounters a current traveling 1.5 meters per second, North. A) What is the resulting velocity of his non-pimped ride? B) If the width of the river is 80 meters wide, what distance downstream does the boat reach the opposite shore? C) There is a buoy in the center of the river. How long will it take Fitzwilliam to reach the buoy from the Southernmost shore?

*(**MARCUS** tries to hand **NATASHA** a calculator. She puts her hand up.)*

NATASHA. So there's like an extra ozone layer on the buoy?

MARCUS. What?

NATASHA. I don't think it's on the buoy at all, and I don't think that this problem is going to contribute to the resolution of that issue or any issue of consequence. Furthermore, I don't drive a motorboat. I don't fraternize with anyone who does. I don't know or care what their resulting velocity is because I have more important things to worry about and quite frankly, so should you.

(light shifts)

Scene Three

(NATASHA leaves the table. LENA creeps behind her and blindfolds her. NATASHA starts to yell.)

LENA. All a game, Tasha – just wait –

NATASHA. Lena –

LENA. It's time for presents.

(LENA drags a box onstage.)

LENA. First you have to guess what's in the box.

NATASHA. I can't.

LENA. You have to.

NATASHA. What's in the box?

LENA. Guess, Tasha.

NATASHA. WHAT'S IN THE BOX?!

LENA. Freak.

(LENA takes out a bottle of perfume and sprays it lightly on NATASHA.)

NATASHA. Your Designer Imposter perfume? Thank you. So much.

LENA. You're welcome. Now it's yours. You get to smell nice.

NATASHA. I smell fine.

LENA. You smell like ink from a Bic pen.

NATASHA. I do not!

LENA. Not now you don't.

(LENA takes out a tiara and puts it on NATASHA's head.)

NATASHA. No.

LENA. But I won it at homecoming.

NATASHA. I hate it.

LENA. You have to love it. You have to keep it, forever and ever –

NATASHA. Give me something I can use.

(**NATASHA** *throws the tiara away as* **LENA** *starts violently brushing her hair.*)

NATASHA. What are you doing – OW –

(**LENA** *takes lipstick out of the box and begins putting it on* **NATASHA**'s *mouth.* **NATASHA** *squirms.*)

LENA. Hold still, Tasha.

NATASHA. I don't wear lipstick –

LENA. I said hold *still*.

(**LENA** *holds* **NATASHA**'s *face firmly and applies the lipstick.*)

LENA. There's some on your teeth. Use your tongue – good girl.

NATASHA. I'm tired of this.

LENA. We're almost done.

(**LENA** *applies blush to* **NATASHA**'s *face, then pulls out a pair of tweezers and starts plucking her eyebrows.*)

NATASHA. That's enough!

LENA. *Fine*, Tasha.

(**LENA** *takes the blindfold off and stands in front of* **NATASHA**.)

LENA. Ta-da!

NATASHA. Shouldn't I have a mirror?

LENA. You don't need one.

NATASHA. I'm done with this. This is stupid.

LENA. You look great. You look just like me.

NATASHA. I don't want to look just like you.

LENA. Are you sure?

(**LENA** *propels* **NATASHA** *forward, into –*)

Scene Four

(NATASHA and MARCUS are studying in the living room.)

NATASHA. ...No, really, I think it's great that you're the kind of person who gets fired up about education – why are you drawing sperm in my notebook?

MARCUS. It's a submarine.

NATASHA. ...That's not a submarine.

MARCUS. You're more of a visual learner so to illustrate –

NATASHA. You're drawing sperm.

MARCUS. That's periscope.

NATASHA. Why is the submarine in a fallopian tube – ?

MARCUS. It's a current.

NATASHA. It looks like a fallopian tube.

MARCUS. Fine. It's a fallopian tube. So we've got a – look – very small submarine moving through a fallopian tube at a speed of –

(MIKE enters.)

MIKE. How's it going?

NATASHA. Marcus is teaching me about fallopian tubes.

MIKE. Okay. Well...hey, look what I rented, for later, if you finish –

(MIKE holds out a copy of a film [determined by the director] that's a favorite of MIKE and NATASHA – she's grown up watching it with her dad, but it might be a little embarrassing now.)

NATASHA. Dad.

MIKE. You and me, after dinner – you finish up your work –

NATASHA. I'm a little bit old –

MIKE. For our tradition? Oh, come on –

(At this point, MIKE cuts loose with a thoroughly dweeby song or quote from the film.)

NATASHA. *Dad.*

MIKE. I'll let you get back to your studying. I'm sure you're doing a great job, Sport.

(**MIKE** *leaves.*)

MARCUS. "Sport?"

NATASHA. What about it?

MARCUS. ...Do you play sports...

NATASHA. Maybe it's wishful thinking. I don't know. He's such a weirdo. He only calls me that to be ironic. He used to get pounded by the jocks, back in the day. I've heard. From my mom. Because she's not a very nice person. But you have to hand it to him. It paid off in the long run. The football guys are probably all pathetic, now, with their spare tires and special cars and mid-life crisis, and my dad has adoring legions. Of frumpy lit major girls, but still.

MARCUS. You've given this a lot of thought.

NATASHA. Not really. Who even knows how you find out what you're good at?

MARCUS. What do you mean?

NATASHA. I don't think he was born with these insights into *The Bell Jar*, how does a guy figure out he has a real flair for teaching women writers? It's like figuring out you know how to peel a banana with your feet. How does that even get started?

MARCUS. Alcohol. You don't know. Maybe he went on a bender one night in college and woke up next to a dog-eared, highlighted copy of *The Joy Luck Club*.

NATASHA. What about you? Did you have a vision?

MARCUS. No. I wanted to be a Marine Biologist. Just like everybody else.

NATASHA. Not everybody wanted to be a marine biologist.

MARCUS. Yes they did. It's universal. It's fact.

NATASHA. I never wanted to be a marine biologist.

MARCUS. You're probably not being honest with yourself.

NATASHA. No. I did not. I never did.

MARCUS. Yes, you did. Every kid did. Every kid wanted to swim with dolphins –

NATASHA. I didn't. I hate them.

MARCUS. Dolphins.

NATASHA. Yes.

MARCUS. You can't hate dolphins.

NATASHA. I can hate anything I want to. It's my constitutional right.

MARCUS. You're practically a terrorist.

NATASHA. Because of the dolphins.

MARCUS. Yes.

NATASHA. I don't like them. I've never liked them. They're annoying.

MARCUS. How are dolphins annoying?

NATASHA. They're so high-pitched! And they bite.

MARCUS. A dolphin bit you?

NATASHA. Not personally. But I've heard. There are stories. About – *violent* dolphin attacks –

MARCUS. When did you realize you were afraid of dolphins – ?

NATASHA. I'm not afraid of dolphins.

MARCUS. It has to come from somewhere. I mean I minored in psychology –

NATASHA. Great, I'll organize a Freudian pride parade just for you, but I never wanted to be a Marine Biologist because I don't like going in the ocean, I don't like getting knocked over by waves, I don't like salt water in my mouth or my ears or my nose and I don't like kelp wrapping around my ankles. How do you know it's just kelp when you're four? How do you know it's kelp now? I wanted to be an astronaut. Which is even more super lame.

MARCUS. Not just regular lame. *Super* lame.

NATASHA. Yeah. I used to hang out in the dryer.

MARCUS. Dryer?

NATASHA. Well – like with the window, you know, it – it's like a command – module – well it is when you're five –

MARCUS. No, that's really imaginative.

NATASHA. It's really stupid, is what it is. My sister used to make so much fun of me –

MARCUS. I didn't know you had a sister.

NATASHA. I do.

MARCUS. Older or younger?

NATASHA. Younger. Just by a year. Just by a little over a year –

MARCUS. She's at school?

NATASHA. No. *(pause)* She left. Really suddenly. She didn't even finish high school.

MARCUS. Oh. You get to see her much –

NATASHA. No. She left.

(LYDIA enters. She makes a noise that alerts NATASHA and MARCUS to her presence.)

LYDIA. Don't let me interrupt you. Don't mind me.

MARCUS. No, we're about done. Anyway, I should get going. Kind of late. See you.

NATASHA. Bye.

(MARCUS exits.)

NATASHA. Starting dinner?

LYDIA. Yes.

(pause)

NATASHA. Can I help? Do you want me to help – ?

LYDIA. No, dear. I'll call you when it's ready.

NATASHA. Mom – It was just that he asked and I don't know why –

LYDIA. I said I'll call you when it's ready.

(NATASHA pauses a moment, then exits.)

Scene Five

(**NATASHA**'s *room.* **NATASHA** *is reading.* **LENA** *sits on the windowsill.*)

LENA. Tasha likes a boy.

NATASHA. No she doesn't.

LENA. I liked a boy one time. More than one. I liked a lot of them, they liked me. Remember that, Tasha? All the boys liked me. More than they liked you. I'm not being mean, I'm just being honest. If I were being mean, I'd tell you what they said about your boobs. They never said it so you could hear, never quite loud enough. They stayed just far enough away because they thought I was pretty, and they knew you were my sister and you still are, Tasha, even if you try to forget.

(**NATASHA** *tries to leave.*)

Mosquito bites, that's what they called them. They were going to bring you a box of band-aids for your mosquito bites but they left you alone because of what happened to me, because you were my sister, and they felt sorry for you. They were sorrier for *you* than they were for *me*.

NATASHA. Lena, be quiet.

LENA. I liked a lot of boys, Tasha, and they liked me, and the one I liked the most was going to ask me to prom. Chris Garcia, with one green eye and the blue one. You know how people's eyes change color when it's cloudy or they're wearing a bright colored shirt? I'd wait for the green to turn blue and the blue to turn green and most of all I'd wait for that second when they'd meet in the middle and I was going to freeze it, that second, it would never belong to anybody but me.

NATASHA. He took Mandy to prom. He had a great time.

LENA. How do you know? You didn't go. You could have gone that year. I was working on it. I was going to go with Chris and make his brother take you. Josh! His skin was almost clear by that time and he was nice. I was going to let you borrow one of my dresses, too, I just hadn't told you yet. I was going to let you borrow my blue one from the year before and I was going to get that green one – we'd have matched Chris' eyes. I wonder if anyone would have noticed.

NATASHA. Probably not.

LENA. And we would have looked so hot in our pictures. The four of us. And we could have driven together and walked in together, that was a good dress, Tasha. It looked okay on me when I wore it the year before but it would have looked *really* nice on you. You would have looked so pretty. And there would be pictures of us. On the mantle, over the fireplace.

NATASHA. I didn't want to go to stupid prom, anyway.

LENA. Maybe not then. But now, you like a boy.

NATASHA. I do not.

LENA. Think he likes you? I mean maybe he does. I don't know. I wouldn't know. I never really hung out with any boys that mom and dad had to pay to come to the house –

NATASHA. Okay, you know what –

LENA. I think you're spending just a little bit too much time thinking about him, Tasha. Don't forget I know what the inside of your head looks like. Kind of scary sometimes.

NATASHA. Whose fault is that – ?

LENA. Fault? We never really talk about that, do we, Tasha, because then there would be all kinds of different questions. You might actually have to think about –

NATASHA. I think about it all the time.

LENA. Really? 'Cause you can't tell. I bet somebody who moved in next door or down the street or something like that might come over here and not think there was anything different, about our family, or about our house. They probably wouldn't think there was anything different all, especially not if they were talking to you –

NATASHA. Mom and Dad are the ones who – especially Mom, she's the one who makes it seem like you never even –

LENA. But you're my sister. You wanna know the first thing I remember? About us?

NATASHA. No.

LENA. The first thing I remember about my sister is us sitting outside and you telling me about the different kinds of stars. About the kinds with two parts, the dark one and the bright one, spinning circles around each other. Binary stars. You were a total dweeb even then.

NATASHA. Right, who's the one using the word "dweeb?"

LENA. Who even thinks of that in the first place? Who looks at the sky and sees a star and thinks, "It has two parts. There's a part you can't see keeping the other one in place."

NATASHA. Giovanni Battista Riccioli. 1650.

LENA. See? Dweeb. I don't like that boy –

NATASHA. Why do you care?

LENA. Because you're my sister. Because it's important. Because you get to be the bright part that everyone sees. You keep me in place and I keep you in place because you said that's how it works, there are two parts and they spin circles around each other. Center of Gravity. That's what you said. And you were, like, five. So it was amazing. And you might be the smart one, but I'm pretty sure you can't just go and change your center of gravity. If we'd have gone that night, the both of us, with Chris and Josh –

NATASHA. You know I never even wanted to go, I always thought prom was lame so I don't know why you keep –

LENA. Because it's nice to imagine. You don't think so? It's not that hard at all, we just pretend that downstairs, on the mantle, over the fireplace, there's not dust. There's a picture.

NATASHA. Lena –

LENA. In the picture, I'm green and you're blue and we're both smiling and nobody has anything in their teeth or shiny skin and we spin circles around each other –

*(**LENA** turns circles around her sister.)*

LENA. We spin circles, at the dance, and everyone watches. Everyone's jealous. Because we're the same. Just for a second. We freeze. With just exactly the same amount of light.

Scene Six

(Dining room. **NATASHA** *is watching* **MARCUS** *review what she's just written.* **LENA** *is supervising.* **NATASHA** *is jumpy.)*

MARCUS. This is mostly right.

NATASHA. Mostly.

MARCUS. Yeah. You just – it's actually three, here, so that –

NATASHA. So it's wrong. It's the wrong answer.

MARCUS. Well, but you had it right up until –

NATASHA. Which would be fine if it were third grade and you got credit for showing the work but since this is a bubble with lead in it, and I only get to pick one –

MARCUS. It's alright –

NATASHA. No, it's not alright, it's also not mostly right. It's incorrect. Here, I'll start over –

MARCUS. So you got one wrong. Even I don't think it's that big a deal. Are you okay?

NATASHA. Yes. I'm fine.

MARCUS. Okay. *(beat)* I only ask because –

NATASHA. I don't need to know why you asked.

MARCUS. Okay. *(beat)* You just seem a little tense, is all –

NATASHA. HOW DO I SEEM TENSE?!

MARCUS. ...Well, I couldn't put my finger on it, exactly. You're making me nervous – with the pen STOP IT. Just – I don't know. Go run around the block ten times or something –

NATASHA. What?

LENA. What did I tell you? He thinks you're FAT.

MARCUS. You just seem really jittery and since we've been sitting here for two hours – I know – come on –

NATASHA. Where.

MARCUS. I want a slushee.

NATASHA. I don't.

MARCUS. Oh.

NATASHA. But I mean I could have a slushee, or, like, watch you have a slushee –

LENA. Riding in cars with boys…

NATASHA. Lena –

MARCUS. Sorry?

NATASHA. Lean…Over there and get me some Advil. Will you? Thank you. I just, um, sometimes you just have ones of those days where there's a high-pitched, annoying little voice in your head and it will not Shut Up –

MARCUS. I'm sorry if I was being too discouraging –

NATASHA. I'm not talking to you. I mean – yes I am – I'm talking to you but I am not talking about you.

MARCUS. I'm never sure. Do you want to go or –

NATASHA. Well – um – you know what, yeah. We should. We should go outside and –

LENA. With the bacteria.

NATASHA. Um –

LENA. That thing we saw on the news that time? Tiny, tiny bacteria, tiny germs, you can't even see them, flesh-eating, mind devouring, crawling on your skin and in your pores and worming under your fingernails –

NATASHA. Gross.

MARCUS. Well, no, they aren't a health food.

NATASHA. What aren't?

MARCUS. Slushees.

NATASHA. No. No, they aren't. Maybe we'd better skip it.

MARCUS. Okay.

LENA. Plus. Slushees make you fat. He already thinks you're fat –

NATASHA. You know what, I think I'm done for the day, I'm sorry. I can't really focus. I'm sorry.

MARCUS. No worries. I'll see you on Tuesday.

NATASHA. Yeah. See you Tuesday.

LENA. Natasha and Marcus, sitting in a tree, f - u - c –

(NATASHA *makes a noise at her sister.* MARCUS *turns around.*)

NATASHA. My head hurts.

MARCUS. Advil?

NATASHA. Good idea.

(NATASHA *sits.* MARCUS *opens the door to leave, but runs into* LYDIA, *who enters with a bag containing boxes of Pan-Asian Cuisine.*)

LYDIA. Marcus, hello –

(LYDIA *hands the boxes to* MARCUS, *who backs up, confused.*)

MARCUS. Hi, Dr. Lisenko –

LYDIA. Nice to see you again. Why don't you join us for dinner?

LENA. No.

NATASHA. Thursdays are MSG night at the Lisenko's.

LENA. No!

NATASHA. No!

(LYDIA *and* MARCUS *look at her.*)

NATASHA. What I mean is of course you should stay if you want to.

MARCUS. I don't want to impose.

LYDIA. Don't be ridiculous –

MIKE. *(entering)* Oh, you're home –

LYDIA. The same. Darling, tell Marcus he has to stay for dinner.

MIKE. Of course he does. There's no excuse unless you're vegan.

MARCUS. I'm not –

(NATASHA *hands* MARCUS *a plate. The four of them dish up and sit down.*)

LYDIA. Natasha, why don't you say grace?

LENA. Grace.

(Everyone bows their head. **LENA** *prevents hand-holding.)*

NATASHA. Lord, for what we're about to receive, please make us truly thankful.

MARCUS, LYDIA, & MIKE. Am –

NATASHA. And also for the immigrant workers paid a dime an hour to prepare it.

ALL BUT NATASHA. Am –

NATASHA. And may I not find hair in my egg roll, like last time.

LENA. Ew.

NATASHA. Amen.

LYDIA. Marcus, I've been meaning to ask you, is tutoring something you plan to do full time? Your mother mentioned that you're starting to have quite a few students –

MARCUS. A good number, yes.

MIKE. So what's next on the horizon?

MARCUS. Well. I think my mother is starting to get tired of me –

LYDIA. I'm sure she's glad to have you back.

MARCUS. But she's used to her space. I would be. So I've been looking at places –

MIKE. I know several very good brokers, Marcus, and I guarantee they'd be willing to cut the fee –

MARCUS. That's really nice of you, Mr. Lisenko – I mean I don't really know exactly, a studio, I guess – just so I can get out of Mom's space.

LYDIA. I just had an idea. A thorough cleaning would be in order, but we have an extra room –

NATASHA. Mom.

LYDIA. It never occurred to me before but if it would help you out, Marcus –

MARCUS. Thank you, but I don't know if –

LYDIA. There's no sense in paying all kinds of fees when we have a perfectly good –

NATASHA. We do not! I'm sorry, Marcus, my mother is a little bit confused. We don't have a spare room.

LYDIA. There's no need for an outburst when all we're doing is discussing, Natasha. Of course it would be temporary. It would be a sublet. Depending on where Natasha gets accepted, if we put the house on the market –

(**NATASHA** *pushes herself away from the table.*)

NATASHA. Excuse me.

LYDIA. You've hardly touched your food.

(**NATASHA** *puts her hands in her food, clears her plate, and exits the room.*)

LYDIA. Michael, I just thought –

MIKE. I think that's enough for right now, Lydia.

LYDIA. Alright. *(pause)* All I was going to say was that –

MIKE. I said that's enough!

LYDIA. Five years, Michael –

MIKE. Do you think you're the only one keeping track?

LYDIA. You know I don't. I just think it's time –

MIKE. For you, maybe. And I don't ask you about it. I don't make you feel like that's somehow inadequate –

LYDIA. But you try, Michael. Do you really think I don't notice –

MIKE. I don't know what to think –

LYDIA. You don't have to agree with me but could you at the very least recognize that I'm the only one who seems to understand that there comes a point when we have to move forward and –

MIKE. Forget.

LYDIA. That's not what I meant and you know it.

MIKE. Please excuse me, Marcus, I've got some papers to grade.

(**MIKE** *exits;* **LYDIA** *remembers* **MARCUS**, *then sets about putting the food away.* **MARCUS** *gets up from the table and helps.*)

Scene Seven

(Several evenings later. **MARCUS** *knocks on* **NATASHA**'s *door, then looks in. He sets something down; he notices the picture on her desk, and then steps to look closer.* **NATASHA** *enters.)*

NATASHA. What are you doing?

MARCUS. Hi – I just – um –

*(***NATASHA** *slams the picture face down.)*

NATASHA. What are you doing here?

MARCUS. Your dad let me in.

NATASHA. Don't change the subject. Is there a good reason you're in my room, pawing at my things –

MARCUS. No, not really.

NATASHA. What are you doing here?

MARCUS. Wishing you luck tomorrow.

NATASHA. Oh.

MARCUS. It's a bad time, though, sorry. I'll –

NATASHA. Marcus, I'm sorry, I shouldn't yell at you, there's no reason for me to yell at you. I should be yelling at my mother except she's not in here and you are and we don't really have a yelling kind of relationship, so, why am I telling you this? Never mind.

MARCUS. Don't be nervous.

NATASHA. …Okay.

MARCUS. I mean about the test.

NATASHA. Okay.

LYDIA. *(off)* Natasha –

NATASHA. Great – That's exactly what I need, right now –

*(***NATASHA** *slams her door.)*

NATASHA. Let me ask you something.

MARCUS. Okay.

NATASHA. Say you have a kid.

MARCUS. I have a kid.

NATASHA. – say your kid is taking a test. Tomorrow. A big deal test. A "what's going to happen with the rest of my life" kind of test.

MARCUS. Okay.

NATASHA. Would that strike you as a good time to make him slash her slash whatever go on down to the DMV and re-take the drive test?

MARCUS. I'm confused.

NATASHA. By the him slash her? I just thought I'd give you options, I mean, it's your imaginary kid –

MARCUS. You don't have a driver's license?

NATASHA. I do, kind of.

MARCUS. How do you kind of have a driver's license?

NATASHA. I had one before. It's not what you think. There was – an incident, with these people, in wheelchairs –

MARCUS. You ran over disabled people?

NATASHA. I tapped them. Lightly. With the fender. They were in wheelchairs, already, so it's not like they were walking – but tell that to the judge, you know? *(pause)* Old people are whiny bitches.

MARCUS. I see.

NATASHA. But anyway, no. I don't technically have a license. I was on probation. It's been bothering my mother. Like, really really bothering her, so finally I just said, "Fine, mom. Let's go on down. Open the gates. Seize the day." She didn't appreciate the reference. She didn't get that I wasn't entirely serious. And she didn't help me by listing the various ways I'd probably screw it up, on the way there. And I messed up just about everything she said I'd mess up. She won't be driving me to the test tomorrow –

MARCUS. You'll do fine.

NATASHA. Whatever. It doesn't really matter.

(beat)

MARCUS. I'm gonna go then.

NATASHA. Okay.

(**MARCUS** *starts to leave.*)

NATASHA. How were you wishing me luck if you didn't think I was here?

MARCUS. Oh – right – also, I was just going to give you this.

(**MARCUS** *hands* **NATASHA** *a cassette tape.*)

NATASHA. A mix tape?

MARCUS. Not really – I just – had these songs that were already – you know, on other tapes and records and CDs –

NATASHA. Oh. Thank you.

MARCUS. I better go –

NATASHA. Yeah, probably.

(**MARCUS** *starts to leave again.*)

NATASHA. But you don't have to. You could listen to the tape with me.

MARCUS. I better not.

NATASHA. Why? Are the songs dirty or something?

MARCUS. I don't think so…it depends on your definition, I guess.

NATASHA. Probably like…Boyz II Men would be –

MARCUS. There's no Boyz II Men on there.

NATASHA. Good. That's good.

MARCUS. Anyway. I hope you like the songs –

NATASHA. I'm sure I will.

(**MARCUS** *starts moving closer.* **NATASHA** *starts moving closer. There's a knock at the door.* **NATASHA** *flails, hitting* **MARCUS** *in the face with her elbow.* **MARCUS** *holds his nose.*)

NATASHA. WHAT WHAT?!

LYDIA. Natasha, are you alright?

NATASHA. I'm great, Mom –

LYDIA. Because you were so upset before.

NATASHA. Well, I'm not upset now.

LYDIA. You sound a little upset.

NATASHA. I have low blood sugar.

LYDIA. Honey, do you want to talk?

NATASHA. Right this second? No.

LYDIA. Because I just feel like we never really get to talk –

NATASHA. We're talking now, Mom! Although I think it would be much better if we set aside some time to talk later –

LYDIA. Oh, you are – you are upset –

NATASHA. No, Mom, I am not upset, I just need some time to –

LYDIA. I didn't mean to come down so hard on you, and neither did your father, but you know how we feel about animals and when you hit that possum –

MARCUS. You hit a possum?

NATASHA. Nobody likes them.

LYDIA. Natasha? Who's in there?

NATASHA. Just Marcus.

LYDIA. Oh, hello, Marcus.

MARCUS. How's it going, Dr. Lisenko?

LYDIA. Just fine.

(*silence*)

LYDIA. What are you doing?

NATASHA. Studying.

LYDIA. Oh. (*pause*) Your math book is out here.

NATASHA. He made up his own bin-packing algorithms.

(**NATASHA** *looks back at* **MARCUS**.)

NATASHA. Stop making a mess.

MARCUS. I'm not doing it on purpose –

LYDIA. What is going on – ?

(**LYDIA** *enters.*)

LYDIA. Oh, Marcus, you're bleeding –

MARCUS. It's just a flesh wound.

NATASHA. It was an accident –

LYDIA. You did this? What happened?

NATASHA. It's not a big deal. I just hit him in the face with my elbow.

LYDIA. How on earth did you manage that?

MARCUS. Yeah, Natasha. How did you manage that?

NATASHA. Shut up.

LYDIA. Natasha! That's no way to behave. Honestly. You know, she's always had the pointiest little elbows –

MARCUS. I can tell.

NATASHA. Mother.

LYDIA. Now, there's no need to be peevish. I have some Midol in my cabinet –

NATASHA. *Mom.*

(**MIKE** *enters.*)

MIKE. What's going on? Oh, hi there, Marcus –

MARCUS. Hi, Dr. Lisenko.

MIKE. What's the problem?

LYDIA. He's clotting, dear. Natasha attacked him.

MIKE. Oh, come on, Sport. Aren't you a little old to be roughhousing?

NATASHA. I assure you, no one was roughhousing in here. Nor are they likely to. *Ever.*

(**NATASHA** *slumps to the floor.*)

MIKE. I think somebody needs to be left alone –

(**MIKE**, **LYDIA**, *and* **MARCUS** *begin to file out.*)

MIKE. You know you have a big day tomorrow, Sport, why don't you turn in early?

NATASHA. Yeah, thanks dad, I think I will.

LYDIA. Now don't forget to put in your bleach trays –

NATASHA. I'm NOT.

LYDIA. They're very expensive and they don't work unless you wear them –

NATASHA. Yeah Mom, thanks. I know.

LYDIA. Here –

NATASHA. MOTHER.

LYDIA. Alright, alright – do you want me to bring you a hot water bottle?

NATASHA. No! I do not.

LYDIA. It's her time of the month.

(NATASHA slams her door. She sighs, puts the tape into the stereo, and presses play. A rock song, something similar to "I Just Don't Know What To Do With Myself" by the White Stripes, plays. NATASHA waits, horrified, for a few moments before turning off the tape and flinging herself onto her bed. LENA crawls out from under it.)

NATASHA. I'm going to kill myself.

LENA. A lot of people would think that's nice, Natasha.

NATASHA. I'm never going outside again.

(A noise outside gets NATASHA's attention.)

NATASHA. Who's out there?

MARCUS. Marcus.

NATASHA. Oh. Hi.

MARCUS. Are you coming out here?

NATASHA. I don't know.

MARCUS. When do you think you'll know?

NATASHA. Um…one second.

(LENA appears.)

LENA. Where are you going? Tasha. Don't go out there. TASHA. Don't go out there. Come on. Think about it. It's like a horror movie.

NATASHA. It's nothing like a horror movie.

LENA. Nobody wants you to go out there. They wouldn't. They'd be watching through their fingers. Doing the silent scream, "No, don't do it, don't do it" – 'cause everybody knows what's going to happen, the same thing that happens every time you think you like some guy, really, Tasha, you're the smart one for a reason. You'd think you'd remember. Plus, look at yourself.

(**NATASHA** *does, but it doesn't produce the desired affect for her sister.*)

LENA. And so what then? Maybe you just feel so good about everything, you do so fabulous on the test –

NATASHA. Fabulous*ly*. I just might do fabulous*ly*.

LENA. Then what? Then you go far away to some big exciting school, in some really big, exciting place, except you hate exciting places and you've never been on a plane because they crash and you're afraid and you've never actually HAD a boyfriend, Tasha, how are you doing to know what do? You won't. You never know what to do. You never know what to say to people. You always say and do the exact thing you wish you hadn't, five seconds after, and then you spend hours and hours thinking about it, how are you going to be around people? How are you going to talk to people? You hate people! You needed me to make everything happen for you, and I did my best and it still wasn't enough. Even though I tried. You forget I know what the inside of your head looks like. I know what you're planning. I don't know how you think you're going to do it though. I don't know how you think you're going to do any of these big exciting things without me.

NATASHA. I'm the smart one, Lena. I'll figure it out.

(**NATASHA** *opens her door and walks to* **MARCUS**. *She's about to kiss him, but them fumbles in her mouth.*)

Bleach trays.

(**NATASHA** *flings her bleach trays to the side. She and* **MARCUS** *kiss.* **LENA** *watches.*)

End ACT ONE

ACT TWO

Scene One

(The past, a memory. **NATASHA** *and* **LENA** *are on the roof.* **NATASHA** *has a toy telescope.)*

LENA. Tasha!

NATASHA. What?

LENA. I just saw a shooting star!

NATASHA. So? I've seen dozens. Hundreds.

LENA. Because you're mean and you never share your telescope.

MIKE. *(offstage)* Girls! Time for bed – school tomorrow.

*(***LENA*** takes the toy away from ***NATASHA***.)*

NATASHA. It already happened, Lena, you can't see it.

LENA. Maybe there will be another one.

NATASHA. Even if there is, it's just a meteoroid. It's not a star at all. It comes into the atmosphere and burns and then disappears. It's just a piece of rock.

LENA. I don't care. I want to make a wish on it.

NATASHA. That's so stupid.

LENA. You don't think it's stupid when you hold your breath on bridges.

NATASHA. That's different.

LENA. Is not. I see the North Star!

NATASHA. You don't. It isn't out tonight.

LENA. Then what's that?

NATASHA. It's Sirius.

LENA. Serious?

NATASHA. It's the brightest star in the whole entire sky and it's really two stars, it has two parts.

LENA. I only see one.

NATASHA. Because the second one is darker.

LENA. How are there two parts to a star?

NATASHA. Because they're really two different stars but we pretend they're the same.

LENA. What if one of them moves?

NATASHA. They can't. Gravitational pull –

LENA. Science words are for dorks. What about when one turns into a black hole like you said?

NATASHA. Not all stars do that.

LENA. Some do.

NATASHA. I guess they'd keep spinning until the one collapsed and ate the other one.

LENA. Stars eat things?

NATASHA. They collapse and spin around and suck things in, like sound, and light, and other stars –

LENA. I saw another one!

NATASHA. You did not.

LENA. You don't know. And I'm not telling you my wish, either.

NATASHA. I don't care.

LENA. Why do some people say shooting and other people call it falling?

MIKE. Lights out in five minutes, girls. I mean it!

NATASHA. I don't know. It's both, I guess; maybe it depends on where you're standing and if it's shooting in Australia then it's falling here.

LENA. Like Lucifer?

NATASHA. Lucifer?

LENA. I'm asking you. In Sunday School they said he was bright like a star –

NATASHA. An angel is different than a star.

LENA. Does he fall or does he shoot?

LYDIA. Girls, brush your teeth.

LENA. Well?

NATASHA. He falls. He definitely falls.

LENA. He's the brightest out of everybody. That's what they say, in the stories. Maybe he was a meteoroid. He was very bright at first and then he moved across the sky and got darker and smaller until you couldn't see him at all?

NATASHA. That's not what happened.

LENA. What did he even do that was so bad?

NATASHA. Something *very* bad, Lena. Something really, really horrible.

LENA. Like picking his nose and eating it?

NATASHA. No.

LENA. Well, I think it's bad *and* horrible and Amy Marshall did it last week and then she tried to *play with my hair,* Tasha. I think she's related to Satan.

NATASHA. He doesn't have relatives. He doesn't even have DNA. Even if he did, it's different because he did something so awful even God couldn't get past it.

LENA. Really awful?

NATASHA. Unforgivable.

LENA. Grown-ups exaggerate, though, Tasha.

NATASHA. I know.

LENA. I bet all he did was wreck the car.

(blackout)

Scene Two

*(The living room. **LYDIA** and **MICHAEL** are opening an envelope as **NATASHA** and **MARCUS** enter.)*

LYDIA. Oh – Natasha, you're back, just in time –

NATASHA. Just in time for what –

MIKE. How was Comicon?

MARCUS. It was great – Sam Raimi was there talking about the special edition release of the trilogy and then Bruce Campell wasn't supposed to be there because if people found out he was there, there'd be a mob scene, but then at the last minute it turned out he was there and had this chainsaw –

NATASHA. They don't actually care. What is that – Mom, that's addressed to me, I told you not to open my mail –

LYDIA. Oh, honey –

NATASHA. "Oh, honey," what. No. You're violating – some amendment, right now.

*(**LYDIA** opens the envelope. She and **MIKE** stare at it before expressing their specific forms of elation.)*

NATASHA. I guess they're going to do this every time I get an acceptance letter.

*(**NATASHA** takes the letter from her parents, then puts it on the table and goes to get a soda.)*

MARCUS. Which one is it?

NATASHA. Yale.

MARCUS. Great.

NATASHA. Yep.

MICHAEL. This is great, Sport. This is the best news yet. I know this is the one you wanted the most –

NATASHA. Really? I didn't know that.

LYDIA. You know, Marcus, this is particularly exciting because Michael and I met at Yale –

NATASHA. Iknowandit'ssuchagoodstorycanyoupleasetellitagain.

LYDIA. I know you were having a hard time deciding, but at least now you know –

NATASHA. Now I know what?

LYDIA. Well, it goes without saying –

NATASHA. Without saying. In case you couldn't tell, Marcus, that's pretty much par for the course around here –

LYDIA. Well, of course you're going to Yale now that you've heard – where else did you propose to –

NATASHA. State.

LYDIA. Why on earth would you go to state?

NATASHA. I don't know.

LYDIA. I don't know, either. You're just being silly – we have to go celebrate –

MIKE. Of course we do – where would you like to go, Sport? Pick anywhere you like.

NATASHA. Chuck E. Cheese.

MIKE. ...I can never tell if she's serious.

LYDIA. Of course she isn't serious. We'll try that new Japanese place Joel and George recommended – how does that sound?

NATASHA. Fine.

MIKE. Marcus, we'd love for you to come, too –

LYDIA. Oh, of course – if you hadn't done such a good job tutoring –

(NATASHA can't help smirking.)

MARCUS. But if you're having a family thing, I don't want to –

NATASHA. No, you should come. You can't leave me alone with them.

LYDIA. I don't think we'll have any trouble getting a table at this hour –

MIKE. No, I don't think so.

LYDIA. I just need a minute to freshen up. You're coming, Marcus?

MARCUS. Yeah. I'll just go set this stuff down.

(**LYDIA** *exits.*)

(*Suddenly for only a second,* **LENA** *is visible to* **NATASHA**. *Her dress is torn. She's dirty. There might be blood.* **NATASHA** *is frozen.* **MARCUS** *and* **MIKE** *notice. Then, just as quickly,* **LENA** *is gone.*)

MARCUS. What is it?

(**NATASHA** *shakes her head and shrugs, and* **MARCUS** *exits.* **MIKE** *has been watching her.*)

MIKE. But you can tell me, right?

NATASHA. What?

MIKE. What is it?

NATASHA. What is what?

MIKE. What's under your skin?

NATASHA. Ligaments, tendons, veins, and bones.

MIKE. You don't seem that excited.

NATASHA. And I should be excited. Lena would have been very, very excited. I mean she always said that's where she wanted to go. I could just stay here and go to State–

MIKE. She wouldn't want you to. She'd want you to get out there, Sport. Lena would want you to be happy.

(**MIKE** *hugs her and exits.* **NATASHA** *glances around for her sister. Nowhere to be found.*)

NATASHA. Want to bet?

Scene Three

(Several weeks later. The living room. **NATASHA** *is organizing a box of photographs and showing them to* **MARCUS** *as she goes along. She keeps glancing around her, without realizing she's doing it.)*

NATASHA. Disgusting…there's something about dusty pictures with greasy fingerprints on them from a decade before…I don't know why she can't go through them herself –

MARCUS. She probably can, she just doesn't want to.

NATASHA. Yeah, pretty much – oh, nasty. What do they want these for? I forgot about this. This is the Halloween I went as the Pythagorean Theorem.

MARCUS. I see.

NATASHA. And here – look at this – Lisenko family vacation, '97. Here we are, raising the roof in front of the Kremlin…this one's pretty much the same only now we're bringing down the house – and then here –

MARCUS. What's that, Disneyland?

NATASHA. No, Marcus, it's Warsaw. You can tell by the large pastel teacups.

MARCUS. Well I knew it was *an* amusement park –

NATASHA. Amusement. Yes. It's all fun and games when you're too young to understand what capitalism is… you'd never know we're smiling at some overweight tourist in a Hawaiian shirt.

MARCUS. Your mom didn't take this picture?

NATASHA. No. This was during the year away.

MARCUS. Year away?

NATASHA. They had trial separations when we were younger. Some longer and some shorter. The nice thing about those is there's no paperwork. And you see how well it all worked out. Oh, look, this is all of us again – here we are on Christmas Eve, setting out milk and cookies for Santa – and here we are setting out bread and vodka for Chekhov –

MARCUS. What?

NATASHA. When you drink, the bread helps soak up –

MARCUS. I know that. Chekhov?

NATASHA. Oh. Right. Well, my dad's always had this thing about embracing our heritage – so when Mom told us about how Santa would come down the chimney and leave presents, I guess my dad got carried away because he told us that if we were good, Chekhov would come down the chimney, too –

MARCUS. And leave what?

NATASHA. The gun in the first act that goes off in the third? I don't know. I just know we'd come in on Christmas morning and look at the big pile of presents…and vodka would be gone. It was magical.

MARCUS. What are you doing?

NATASHA. …Sorting pictures.

MARCUS. No, you keep looking around. You keep looking over your shoulder –

NATASHA. I do?

MARCUS. You've been doing it all week.

NATASHA. Oh. I don't know. It's just quieter than usual without my parents, maybe it makes me nervous. It's kind of like Manderly, isn't it?

MARCUS. What is?

NATASHA. Our house.

MARCUS. Manderly is –

NATASHA. Nothing. Never mind. It's from a book.

*(She continues sorting the pictures. **MARCUS** sits next to her. They start kissing, but **NATASHA** isn't feeling it. She fumbles for the remote control and turns on the television, still while kissing **MARCUS**. A familiar theme plays.)*

NATASHA. HEY.

MARCUS. …What.

NATASHA. Nova!

*(**NATASHA** turns up the sound.)*

MARCUS. It's a re-run.

NATASHA. How do you know?

MARCUS. Because it's been on for thirty years. It's *always* a re-run.

NATASHA. It's a good one. It's about…quarks.

(The phone rings. **NATASHA** *reaches for it. She answers and sits back down with* **MARCUS.***)*

NATASHA. Hello? Hi, Daddy…I'm great. That's great. No. Don't hurry back if you don't want to – Yes, he's here. *(long silence)* Actually, Dad, that's exactly what we've been doing. Completely unprotected. Heh. – my Dad says hi – …uh-huh…Well – probably – what? I – hi, Mom…No, the burners aren't on. Why would they be on? Well – sure I've *used* them – no, I don't feel like it. No! Because I don't *want* to. Because I happen to be extremely comfortable right now…my mom says hi, too – what? Mother, I'm telling you. The burners are not on right now. None of them. Because I *know*. Mom, I – fine. Fine!

*(***NATASHA** *gets up from the couch and goes toward the kitchen.)*

NATASHA. I'm checking, right now – I said I'm *checking* –

(The doorbell rings. **NATASHA** *motions for* **MARCUS** *to answer it, then goes into the kitchen.* **MARCUS** *gets up. There's a knock.* **MARCUS** *opens the door to reveal a man in a suit.)*

MARCUS. Can I help you?

LIEUTENANT HARRIS. Is Mr. Lisenko at home?

MARCUS. Sorry, no he's not –

LIEUTENANT HARRIS. Mrs. Lisenko?

MARCUS. She's not here either, they're on vacation –

LIEUTENANT HARRIS. I see. You're the housesitter?

MARCUS. No, I'm a friend of their daughter's.

LIEUTENANT HARRIS. Natasha's home right now? She didn't go with them?

MARCUS. No. She's here.

LIEUTENANT HARRIS. Do you have any idea when Mr. and Mrs. Lisenko will be home – ?

MARCUS. This coming Friday, I think. Natasha has the number, if you need to –

(**NATASHA** *re-enters the room. Stops when she sees* **LIEUTENANT HARRIS.**)

NATASHA. Lieutenant Harris.

LIEUTENANT HARRIS. Hello, Natasha.

NATASHA. Hello.

(silence)

NATASHA. This is my friend, Marcus.

LIEUTENANT HARRIS. He tells me that your parents are on vacation?

NATASHA. They're in Cabo. My dad just got promoted, tenure, I mean. They haven't been on a trip in a long time. They're celebrating. They'll be back Friday.

LIEUTENANT HARRIS. I heard.

NATASHA. Can I get you something to drink? We have soda or juice or water if you want –

LIEUTENANT HARRIS. No, thank you. I'd hoped to speak with your parents –

NATASHA. Well, they aren't here. They'll be back on Friday. I just talked to them. I just got off the phone. They went parasailing. They said they hoped I wasn't jealous. I've always wanted to go parasailing – They'll be home on Friday – they're flying into Oakland, flight 238, 1:55 pm, terminal 7 – this Friday, they'll be home –

LIEUTENANT HARRIS. There's been a break on your sister's case.

(**LENA** *appears. She should look normal, exactly as she did in the first scene.*)

LENA. You don't have to listen to him.

LIEUTENANT HARRIS. There's no easy way for me to do this, Natasha – I don't know how to express how deeply, deeply sorry –

*(**LIEUTENANT HARRIS** seems to continue to speak, though **LENA** drowns out both he and **MARCUS** for **NATASHA**, and the audience.)*

LENA. I don't like him. He's making things up and you shouldn't listen to him. You should listen to me. I know we haven't talked in a while. I was mad at you. It's not very nice to go places and do things without even telling your sister, first, but I forgive you. I think.

LIEUTENANT HARRIS. – anonymous call from a hiker in Muir Woods –

LENA. Yale. What a big, big deal. Big, swinging deal, that's what Dad used to say. Well, he's right. It is a big deal. I don't know what your problem is. I'd have been really excited about it. You were right when you said that. You were so right.

LIEUTENANT HARRIS. – positive identification –

LENA. I hate him. You should make him leave. We should ignore him. We should go outside and we should make-believe that it's like before and we're the two parts of the star spinning around together, the dark and the light, and when you can't see the one you can see the other, and they just keep spinning in each other's circles, and they never spin loose and they never get free.

LIEUTENANT HARRIS. – dental records show that –

LENA. See why I hate him? He's like everybody else. He's trying to make you forget me. Why do you think people put things in boxes and cover them with dirt? So they don't have to see and they're allowed to forget, but you won't forget me, Tasha –

LIEUTENANT HARRIS. – tracking a number of suspects –

LENA. You *won't*. You won't get away and neither will I because we're the two parts of the star, and everybody who looks thinks they only see one but that's why the star is so *bright*, Tasha, because there's always the two of them, the light and the dark, and they aren't in the orbit of anything else, it's just them and their circles and the shadows they make for each other and it's enough, it's enough, and they take turns hiding in each other's shadows –

NATASHA. So you want me to look at what? What's at the station? What is it that I'm going to see?

LIEUTENANT HARRIS. ...Natasha, you misunderstood me – There's no need for that. We've already verified that – You don't need to see.

NATASHA. People get files mixed up, all the time, and you don't know – if you can't even – if you saw and you couldn't even tell, there's a million different people it could be –

LENA. That's right, Tasha, millions and billions and gazillions –

NATASHA. It could be someone else –

LIEUTENANT HARRIS. I'm so sorry.

NATASHA. It could be someone else!

LIEUTENANT HARRIS. Natasha – your bracelet. Your sister also had –

NATASHA. She never wore it –

LIEUTENANT HARRIS. But –

(NATASHA *takes off her own bracelet and throws it on the floor.* LENA *takes hers off and sets it next to* NATASHA*'s.*)

LENA. It's okay. Now neither of us have them.

NATASHA. I'll be there in half an hour.

LIEUTENANT HARRIS. That isn't necessary.

NATASHA. It'll take me about half an hour. Are there things I can do so my parents don't have to? They're out of the country. Are there some things I can do –

LIEUTENANT HARRIS. Yes, but –

NATASHA. Okay, then, I'll be right there.

(LIEUTENANT HARRIS *exits.*)

LENA. You can't forget about me.

Scene Four

(Several weeks later. **LYDIA** *is sitting at the dining room table, with a calculator and an array of papers.* **MARCUS** *enters, with wallet, on his way to the door.)*

LYDIA. Hello, Marcus –

MARCUS. How's it going?

LYDIA. Taxes are taxes, but I'm powering through – I usually just have Michael do them, but he's got so many more papers to grade these days –

MARCUS. I'm going to the corner for Natasha really quick, do you need anything?

LYDIA. No, thank you. *(pause)* What am I saying? We're out of milk, actually, we need milk – only now I can't for the life of me remember where I put my wallet – I'll just run out and get it later.

MARCUS. I've got it.

LYDIA. No, Marcus, that's not necessary –

MARCUS. I don't mind. I'll be there anyway.

LYDIA. I'll find it the minute you leave – I'll have the money for you, when you get back –

MARCUS. Dr. Lisenko, it's fine. It's milk.

LYDIA. Marcus, how many times have I told you to call me Lydia?

MARCUS. …A lot of times?

LYDIA. That's right.

MARCUS. I'll be right back.

*(***MARCUS*** exits.* **LYDIA** *sets busily to work again. She works for a moment, reaches a certain point on the page in front of her. She takes off her glasses and starts to cry.* **MARCUS** *re-enters.)*

MARCUS. I forgot to ask what kind you –

*(***MARCUS*** notices* **LYDIA**'s *face, and stops.* **LYDIA** *straightens up and puts her glasses back on.)*

MARCUS. Are you –

LYDIA. I'm fine. Thank you. Nonfat. Please.

MARCUS. Okay.

(Neither of them moves.)

LYDIA. Just a stupid mistake I made – you have to pay attention on these – this is why Michael usually does them.

*(**LYDIA** methodically covers a spot on the paper with whiteout.)*

LYDIA. You always do this, everyone does, you file dependants – I wasn't paying attention – you file dependents, you file children, and instead of one I wrote two. And it's *pen*.

*(**MARCUS** sits next to **LYDIA**.)*

LYDIA. Everyone knows you don't use pen.

*(**LYDIA** cries on **MARCUS**' shoulder. He tries to arrange himself less awkwardly. **NATASHA** enters. She stares at **MARCUS** and her mother for a moment.)*

NATASHA. Should I leave you guys alone?

*(**MARCUS** jumps up.)*

MARCUS. I was just going.

*(**MARCUS** leaves. **NATASHA** takes out a box of cereal, opens the refrigerator, and stares in.)*

NATASHA. We don't have milk?

LYDIA. No, we don't. Marcus just said he'd get some.

*(**NATASHA** takes the cereal to the couch, collapses onto it, and begins flipping channels while eating the cereal out of the box. **LYDIA** watches her.)*

LYDIA. Marcus is really good to you, isn't he?

NATASHA. I don't know. It's kind of pathetic.

*(**LYDIA** continues to stare at her daughter. **NATASHA** pretends to ignore this and turns the volume up as high as it can go. An obnoxious theme from a children's program blares.)*

LYDIA. Could you please turn that down?

NATASHA. Sorry, what?

LYDIA. Could you turn it down? I'm trying to work.

NATASHA. Sorry, can't hear you!

LYDIA. Will you turn that down –

NATASHA. Do you mind? I'm trying to watch this –

*(**MIKE** walks through the door, tired, briefcase in one hand, a stack of mail under his arm. **NATASHA** mutes the television.)*

NATASHA. Hi, Daddy.

MIKE. Hi, Tasha.

*(The use of name makes **NATASHA** turn. **MIKE** absently kisses **NATASHA**, then **LYDIA**, and spreads the mail out on the table, sorting it.)*

LYDIA. How was your day, darling?

MIKE. The same. What about yours?

LYDIA. I'm almost done with this.

MIKE. On your day off, too – I was going to get around to it.

LYDIA. But now you don't have to, you can just relax.

MIKE. Well, I appreciate it.

(sorting the mail)

Sprinkler repair –

LYDIA. Already dealt with.

MIKE. Various catalogues –

LYDIA. Just set them to the side.

MIKE. Card.

LYDIA. From who?

MIKE. Melissa and David.

*(**MIKE** opens the card and scans the contents.)*

LYDIA. It seems like I never run into Melissa. I should call her one of these days.

MIKE. Yes. Call her and thank her for the lovely, thought out sympathy card.

(**LYDIA** *reaches out for the card, but* **MIKE** *withholds it.*)

MIKE. Rite Aid, looks like. $2.99. What do you think, Sport?

NATASHA. About what?

MIKE. You remember Mrs. Anderson –

NATASHA. One of mom's friends, right?

MIKE. That's right. Now tell me, how long do you think it took Mom's friend Mrs. Anderson to pick out this card? Keep in mind it was probably somewhere in the middle of the list, in between picking up toilet paper and dropping off film.

NATASHA. Um…I don't know.

MIKE. Well, considering that the poem inside would seem to have been composed by a third grader –

LYDIA. Michael.

MIKE. With a learning disability –

LYDIA. Honestly.

MIKE. I'm only stating it for the record, Lydia. Let's see what Natasha thinks. Sport, do you think the words "could" and "world" rhyme?

NATASHA. No.

LYDIA. What would you like for dinner?

MIKE. Here we have a signature. Underneath the "poem." These people couldn't bring themselves to write a message –

LYDIA. These people are our friends, Michael. Natasha, why don't you help me in the kitchen?

MIKE. "The Anderson Family." If memory serves me correctly, Melissa and Dave have children.

LYDIA. You know they do, Michael.

MIKE. What are their names; I'm drawing a blank –

NATASHA. Chelsea and Taylor, Dad.

MIKE. Right. And about how old are Chelsea and Taylor these days?

NATASHA. I think they're in high school. Why does it matter?

MIKE. It doesn't. Not really. There's no reason they should be bothered to sign the card, there's no use for anything beyond one person scrawling "The Anderson Family" at the bottom of this – can you really call it a poem? I can't.

LYDIA. Veal cutlets? Or spaghetti.

MIKE. There's no reason at all. $2.99 is perfectly sufficient. It's only our daughter's body, in the woods –

LYDIA. Michael. Goddamn it.

(LYDIA starts slamming plates down. MARCUS re-enters.)

LYDIA. This is the end of this discussion. Who would like to set the table?

MIKE. I can see it right now, Lydia, Melissa Anderson's shopping list.

LYDIA. I will. Nevermind. It's no trouble at all!

MIKE. Batteries, ink cartridge, and right in the middle, a card for the people whose daughter needed dental records to be identified.

LYDIA. What would you like to drink, Marcus? Water, juice, milk, or ginger ale?

MIKE. Send them a nice note, Lydia, or better yet, drop them a line.

LYDIA. They mean well, Michael.

MIKE. You can't mean well if you don't mean it to begin with. I'm sure they'd like to. I'm sure they tried. They might care, Lydia, they might care exactly two dollars and ninety-nine cents worth – plus sales tax – but they can't mean it because they can't understand unless it's their daughter in pieces in a bag. And one of these days I almost hope it is.

LYDIA. *Michael.*

NATASHA. Daddy.

MIKE. I hope it is.

(MIKE exits. Blackout.)

Scene Five

*(**NATASHA**'s room, night. **NATASHA** is sleeping in bed. Something climbs over her – **LENA**, dress torn, hair matted, bloody, cold, afraid. **LENA** has a knife.)*

LENA. Bitch.

*(**LENA** drags the knife along the pillow on the right side of **NATASHA**'s head.)*

LENA. Slut.

*(**LENA** runs the knife along the other side.)*

LENA. Whore.

*(**LENA** pushes the blade against **NATASHA**'s throat. **NATASHA** wakes up and **LENA** stifles her scream.)*

LENA. It sounds funny, doesn't it? Coming out of some little girl? That's all I was to him. Some girl. Some ass. You know.

*(**LENA** presses the knife harder.)*

LENA. *You* know.

*(**NATASHA** squirms.)*

LENA. Say please. Say it.

*(**LENA** uncovers **NATASHA**'s mouth.)*

NATASHA. Please –

*(**LENA** covers **NATASHA**'s mouth again.)*

LENA. Say it like you mean it! Like I said it.

*(**LENA** uncovers **NATASHA**'s mouth.)*

NATASHA. *Please.*

LENA. Over and over, and all I could think of was you, at home, and how you'd be waiting for me. Mom, and Daddy, but mostly you. Remember this dress? You were with me when I bought it and I screamed when he tore it. I said please, please, please, and then suddenly I couldn't see him over me anymore, I just saw Mom and Daddy and Tasha, sitting at the table. You were looking at the clock. Mom asked you where I was and you said you didn't know. Isn't that right, Tasha? Isn't that how it happened?

NATASHA. Please.

LENA. I kept saying it and saying it. And I turned my head and I saw the light of our house through the trees in the park, and I knew you were inside, you were safe, you were warm, and I was caught between the trees and I tasted my blood, but I knew I wouldn't hate you, Tasha, because I love you, you're my sister.

(LENA kisses NATASHA's forehead.)

You're my sister.

(LENA kisses NATASHA again, next to her mouth.)

LENA. But you have to ask forgiveness.

NATASHA. I'm sorry.

LENA. What?

NATASHA. I'm sorry!

LENA. You're sorry for what, Tasha?

NATASHA. I'm *sorry* –

LENA. You have to start back at the beginning! Say it! Say it so everybody can hear, everybody in the world, everybody who read the papers, and all the police, and all of our friends, and mom and, and dad.

(knock at the door)

MIKE. Sport? What's happening in there, are you alright?

NATASHA. Lena –

LENA. They won't love you and you know I'm right.

NATASHA. I didn't mean to – I didn't –

LENA. I bet they won't now, Tasha. They're not like I am. I love you even after what you did.

(pounding at the door)

LYDIA. Open the door, Natasha, we're getting worried –

LENA. Right now, Tasha.

NATASHA. I can't.

LENA. Right *now.*

MIKE. Natasha, we're coming in –

LENA. Say it right now or I'll never, ever forgive you!

(**MIKE** *and* **LYDIA** *force the door open.*)

NATASHA. I made her walk!

(**MIKE** *and* **LYDIA** *stand still, uncomprehending.*)

NATASHA. I made her walk home.

Scene Six

(A beach, night. **NATASHA** *is sitting on the ground, drawing in the sand, singing to herself. Behind her,* **MARCUS** *approaches holding two slushees.* **NATASHA** *notices him and takes one.)*

NATASHA. This is red.

MARCUS. I know –

NATASHA. I told you I don't like red.

MARCUS. They didn't have blue. The machine was broken, or something. They didn't have the kind you wanted so I made a guess – it's cherry.

NATASHA. It's *red*.

MARCUS. Right, but it's cherry-flavored and the kind you like, I'm guessing, is blue-cherry flavored –

NATASHA. No, it isn't. It's just blue.

MARCUS. It can't be just blue.

NATASHA. ...How could anyone even know that? You don't know that, you're just –

MARCUS. No, but I'm saying the kind you like is probably blue cherry –

NATASHA. I've only ever said I wanted a blue slushee and I've gotten –

MARCUS. Well, it has to have some kind of artificial fruit flavor.

NATASHA. No, it doesn't. If you go to 7-11 they have Coca-cola slushees and that's not any kind of fruit flavor –

MARCUS. It's either blue cherry or blue raspberry, the kind you usually get. So there's a fifty-fifty chance that I got you the same flavor, it's just a different color. You're welcome.

NATASHA. ...Stain my tongue red –

MARCUS. The other would stain your tongue blue.

NATASHA. It's a matter of preference...

(quiet)

NATASHA. What did they say?

MARCUS. Who?

NATASHA. Who do you think, my parents. What did they say to you about getting me out of the house? I just didn't figure the impromptu field trip was your idea –

MARCUS. You want to leave?

NATASHA. No. I don't know. Whatever. It's kind of a good thing.

MARCUS. What is?

NATASHA. Air. Does our house smell and no one's telling us?

MARCUS. What?

NATASHA. Never mind.

MARCUS. Your house doesn't smell –

NATASHA. No, I just mean – we don't – my mom doesn't – the windows – never mind. I don't know what I meant.

(quiet)

MARCUS. Hey, do you want to go on a trip?

NATASHA. …What kind of trip?

MARCUS. Like to Montana.

NATASHA. Probably not but, um, thanks for asking. I think.

MARCUS. No, it's just um – my dad, and my stepmom, they're there – in Montana, right –

NATASHA. Right. You told me.

MARCUS. Apparently they have this kid now. Like from Poland.

NATASHA. Oh.

MARCUS. They didn't really tell anyone until it was official and – so I guess it's there, now, and so there's kind of a – thing, I guess, that they want to have for everybody to come and look at it –

NATASHA. Look at it.

MARCUS. Because it can't sit up or talk yet. Nothing like that. It's not an infant because those are a lot more expensive but it's still –

NATASHA. Still counts as a baby.

MARCUS. Yeah.

NATASHA. Well, that's great. That's really nice. Um…congratulations to them. If you talk to them.

MARCUS. Well, he invited you –

NATASHA. The mute baby from Poland?

MARCUS. It's a girl. No, um, my dad. And Cheryl. That's my stepmom –

NATASHA. I know that. You told me.

MARCUS. It's totally fine if you don't want to, or if you do, I just thought if you did we should probably figure out tickets –

NATASHA. Tickets –

MARCUS. Plane tickets.

NATASHA. I don't go on planes.

MARCUS. You have to go on a plane sometime. If you're going to go to Yale –

NATASHA. I can't go on a plane. I've been on one plane, exactly one time. It was horrible. We hit this turbulence –

MARCUS. There's always that –

NATASHA. No, it was *horrible*. There were oxygen masks. This guy started reading from – Revelation or something, I don't know – the lights were flickering –

MARCUS. It happens.

NATASHA. I blacked out. I had to be revived. Apparently that's what happens if you hold your breath for too long. Fade to black. Of course I wasn't thinking about making sure oxygen got to my brain, I just thought if I held my breath I could keep the plane in the sky. I always had a pretty good track record. Like when you go past a cemetary. Don't breathe. Or else you might breathe in a dead person. And… bridges, and tunnels. I always hold my breath on bridges and in tunnels and none of them have ever collapsed in on me or fallen apart underneath me…

MARCUS. We were talking about Montana.

NATASHA. Right. It was very nice of them to invite me, Marcus, and please thank them when you talk to them. But it sounds like a family thing. I don't think that I should go.

MARCUS. Okay. But they would like to meet you –

NATASHA. Why? What did you tell them?

MARCUS. That I have a girlfriend and –

NATASHA. You say girlfriend?

MARCUS. What do you say? When you talk to people –

NATASHA. I don't talk to people. I'm just curious to know what you told them about me –

MARCUS. Um…not a lot, really –

NATASHA. Right. I don't blame you.

MARCUS. Can you not –

NATASHA. Because then you'd have them wondering what's wrong with *you*. I don't think you want that. And I guarantee you they would, you tell them you're dating a hermit, who can't drive –

MARCUS. Natasha –

NATASHA. She's funny. She does have that going for her. But there again it doesn't cancel out this one incident where she sort of killed her sister –

MARCUS. Stop.

NATASHA. But that's actually kind of a funny story, too, not the body in the woods part, but the irony of it, if you could call it that. There are traces of irony, just hints. Like you find hints of a struggle. Like you find blood on a rock. Like you find hair on the ground. Like you find a piece, a remnant of a sweater –

MARCUS. Stop it.

NATASHA. Not until you listen.

MARCUS. I listen all the time.

NATASHA. A SWEATER. Not even a great sweater. A sweater that looks like any other sweater in any other store for boring middle class people to shop in. Nothing special about the sweater, but it's mine, right? It belongs to me.

And she takes it, again, and she doesn't ask. She never asks about anything. She never asks to take the car. We're supposed to be sharing it but of course that day is like any other day. She leaves before I do, with the car, so that I have to walk and I don't even see that she's wearing my sweater until we pass each other in the hall between third period and fourth. She knows I'm angry. She looks right through me. Flips her hair and just keeps talking to the boys who are following her. Boys are always following her. I take my seat in science. I wait until I know she's in the gym, playing basketball. I pretend that I'm using the hall pass to get a drink of water but instead I go into the locker room and get the keys out of her backpack. We don't see each other again until the parking lot after school. She sees me leaving. She says she needs the car because she has yearbook. She has to stay late. She yells at me. Says I'm selfish. I roll up the window, I play my song. I drive away. And I can't blame them, my parents. I would hate me, too.

MARCUS. Your parents don't hate you –

NATASHA. Yes! They do! they should.

MARCUS. Can we just stop talking about this? Please. For – five minutes, ten minutes – It's all I ever hear about, it's all you ever talk about.

NATASHA. Okay, then. Why don't we drive to Montana and listen to The Electric Company the whole way there. Sunshine and rainbows for everybody!

MARCUS. I don't know what to tell you. Maybe you're right. Maybe it is your fault. Isn't that what you want to hear? Because I don't know why else you'd keep saying it over and over, because even you have to understand people are only going to disagree with you so many times –

NATASHA. Even me? Even a crazy hermit who can't drive has to understand –

MARCUS. I changed my mind, you're right. It is your fault, all your fault. She's dead because you killed her, because you knew she'd take the shortcut. You knew what would happen. I told my parents, I have this girlfriend now. I really like her. We like all the same things. She's smart, she's funny, she's way too pretty to be with me. But she's not as pretty as her sister was. She'll never be like her sister. That's why she killed her. That's why she made her walk home, through the woods, on purpose. *(pause)* That's what you want me to say, isn't it? That's what you want someone to say. Just so you can fight back.

NATASHA. My family used to have four people in it, now it has three. Do you wonder why the furniture is different in our house every time you come in? Because my mother can't stop rearranging it. She can't stop trying not to make the house look empty. Every room is too big. My mother can't stop trying to cover up the holes in the walls and the floor with different pictures and rugs or mats, you can't see them, but they're there. Our house is filled with holes. And so are we. Because of what I did.

MARCUS. I can't see you any more.

*(Beat. **NATASHA** gently covers his eyes with her hands.)*

NATASHA. So don't.

MARCUS. What did you want from me?

*(**NATASHA** uncovers his eyes)*

NATASHA. The right kind of slushee.

Scene Seven

*(Dim light in **NATASHA**'s room, which is in disarray. When the light comes up on **NATASHA**'s room, she is a near coma-case, on her bed, mouthing the words to the song she's listening to. **LENA** is observing this. **NATASHA** can't see or hear **LENA**.)*

LENA. What is this?

*(**NATASHA** doesn't hear her.)*

LENA. Sick. I'm sorry. I hate to have to get all Patrick Swayze in *Ghost* in here but –

*(**LENA** snaps. The music shuts off. **NATASHA** gets up to investigate the problem, but gets up too quickly, and is dizzy.)*

LENA. Oh…Not getting our vital nutrients these days, are we, sissy?

*(**NATASHA** reaches for a can of whipped cream that's lying on the floor. She's about to squirt it into her mouth, but then catches sight of a bag of potato chips. She considers the two options, then puts the whipped cream on the potato chip and eats it. She still can't hear or see her sister.)*

LENA. This is pathetic. It's even worse than the time Paul Ashley went out with her for two days in seventh grade and then dumped her and then later she found out it was part of a science project. Like, literally. She went on a hunger strike and moved into a tent in the backyard for a week and a half.

(There's a noise outside.)

LENA. I hear footsteps approaching!

(There's a knock at the door.)

NATASHA. *(mouth full)* What, Mom –

MARCUS. It's me.

*(**NATASHA** panics, doesn't know what to do about her personal appearance.)*

LENA. You know that saying, "Looking good is the best revenge?" My sister doesn't.

(**NATASHA** *opens the door.* **MARCUS** *enters, holding a DVD set.*)

MARCUS. Hi.

NATASHA. Hi.

MARCUS. I thought you'd want this back.

NATASHA. Oh. Thanks.

MARCUS. No problem. How've you been?

NATASHA. Fine. You?

MARCUS. Yeah.

LENA. What's the matter with you? Go. Fetch. Haven't you been trying to telepathically *summon* him to come over here?

MARCUS. So…

NATASHA. What?

MARCUS. Nothing.

NATASHA. Oh.

LENA. You guys are so boring. I swear to God. I have to do everything. You guys need some mood music.

(**LENA** *snaps and the "Pas de Deux" from "The Nutcracker" starts playing.* **NATASHA** *rubs her head.* **LENA** *starts to dance.*)

MARCUS. Are you alright?

NATASHA. Yeah, I just…Have this weird headache all of the sudden – Do you hear anything?

MARCUS. No.

NATASHA. Okay…

LENA. This is perfect. Remember when Daddy and Mom first took us to see this and I was so excited about the Sugarplum Fairy that I asked for ballet lessons for Christmas and they wanted you to be graceful so they made you take them to?

NATASHA. So – Thanks for dropping it by –

MARCUS. Oh, yeah, of course – I wanted to come and see you, too, because I'm actually leaving sooner than I thought –

NATASHA. You're –

MARCUS. I'm doing that teaching thing – in Tokyo –

NATASHA. Right –

MARCUS. And I'm just leaving sooner.

NATASHA. How much sooner?

MARCUS. Tomorrow.

NATASHA. Oh. Okay.

LENA. And then they held you back for three years, so when you were eight, you were dancing with five year olds, and finally Mom felt sorry for you and let you quit.

NATASHA. I'm leaving, too.

MARCUS. You are? I mean – that's great. Okay. Where did you decide to – ?

NATASHA. Yale. And we're moving.

MARCUS. Oh – where –

NATASHA. I'm going to New Haven. My mother is taking a job in Seattle. My dad is staying here.

MARCUS. I'm sorry.

NATASHA. I don't really care.

MARCUS. Are you sure you're alright?

NATASHA. Yes, I just feel like I'm hearing this music and it's just really *loud* –

LENA. Because it's like the greatest song *ever*. It's so pretty and sad and out of place in a story about a girl who's obsessed with a giant walnut-cracking device.

MARCUS.	**NATASHA.**
About before, I –	I've really been wanting to –

MARCUS. Go ahead.

NATASHA. No, you first.

MARCUS. That's alright.

NATASHA. No. Really. You go first.

MARCUS. You.

NATASHA. I don't have anything to say.

MARCUS. Neither do I.

LENA. Tasha, come on.

NATASHA. Be quiet.

MARCUS. …I am quiet.

NATASHA. Wait, what?

MARCUS. You just told me to be quiet.

NATASHA. I…didn't mean to… I don't know who I was talking to. I'm really out of it. I'm sorry.

MARCUS. So I'll see you.

NATASHA. Yeah. See you.

*(**MARCUS** gives **NATASHA** a hug, then leaves.)*

LENA. And she watches him leave. Like you do. Then he goes downstairs, and she listens to him leave, but only at first, because the stairs are carpeted, so halfway down she tries to sense him leaving, which besides being not actually possible is also totally pathetic.

*(**NATASHA** crosses to the window.)*

LENA. Then he's outside and she can see him walking towards the car, and she knows it's her one, great, big chance to be like Ingrid Bergman and change the ending of *Casablanca*. And it's just waiting there, hovering in the back of her throat – like when you drink soda but you keep your mouth shut and so the carbonation comes out your nose – and this, this she does not want hurtling through her nasal passage, so she calls out –

NATASHA. Marcus!

LENA. And he turns, and for a second it's all hanging there between the second story window and the lawn under his sneakers, every single, possible turn this story could take. And what does my sister choose? What, out of the infinite thousands of possibilities, does my sister the smart one choose to say?

NATASHA. Stay mellow!

(**NATASHA** *hits herself and then goes tearing through a notebook.*)

LENA. It's not over yet, though, because she's got it all written down, everything she needs to say, and somehow, with only a little paraphrasing, it just fits on one front-back piece of loose-leaf.

(**NATASHA** *rips out the piece of paper and goes back to the window.*)

NATASHA. Marcus!

LENA. But he's in his car.

NATASHA. *Marcus!*

LENA. With the radio blaring.

NATASHA. Marc –

(**NATASHA** *looks down at the piece of paper and starts folding it into a paper airplane.*)

LENA. He's having trouble starting his engine and the passenger side window is cracked just enough to allow one airplane of approximately one inch high and four inches wide to enter and hit him in the side of the head, provided the distance, angle and speed of departure, temperature, and wind velocity all convene in just the right way.

(**NATASHA** *throws the airplane.*)

LENA. And if the neighbor's stupid dog didn't happen to run across the yard right then and also happen to love playing catch, and if my sister weren't too stubborn – who knows what might have been?

(**NATASHA** *flops into bed.* **LENA** *does the "dying swan" pose as the music comes to a dramatic end.*)

LENA. And the village went to sleep for a hundred years.

Scene Eight

(LENA's room, untouched and exactly the same as it appeared five years before. It's the bedroom of a popular 17 year-old cheerleader. NATASHA stands in the doorway, backpack at her side. The shades are drawn and it's dark, even though it's mid-day. After a moment she opens a drawer and pulls out a sweatshirt, which she presses against herself and smells. LYDIA stands in the doorway.)

LYDIA. Your father is ready.

NATASHA. I thought you were both taking me.

LYDIA. I have some work to catch up on; besides, you don't want both of your parents making a scene at the airport. I'm sure your father will have that aspect covered –

NATASHA. Mom.

LYDIA. He's ready, he said to tell you; he's downstairs. I can't imagine why these shades are drawn –

NATASHA. Mom –

(LYDIA opens the shades.)

LYDIA. Isn't that much nicer?

(LYDIA looks at the sweatshirt. NATASHA ties it around her waist.)

LYDIA. Do you have everything?

NATASHA. I think so.

LYDIA. Well – you'd have loved the reactions I got when I told everyone at work your news.

NATASHA. Why do you have to tell everyone?

LYDIA. Because we're proud of you, darling. We're both very proud of you.

MIKE. *(offstage)* Sport, let's go!

LYDIA. You don't want to miss your flight.

NATASHA. It isn't for five hours.

LYDIA. You never know – traffic delays –

NATASHA. Still.

(NATASHA *tightens the sweatshirt.*)

NATASHA. Mom, I'm sorry.

LYDIA. Now, you will call as soon as you land –

NATASHA. Mom.

LYDIA. Aren't you glad you have a direct flight? I always hated changing – besides there's less of a chance your luggage will get misplaced –

NATASHA. Mom.

LYDIA. I'll never forget the time that happened to me – it was the second semester of my freshman year and I was miserable trying to make do with the things in my overnight bag –

NATASHA. I'm sorry.

LYDIA. My advice is not to sleep at all on the flight, and to drink lots of water – I've never tried it myself yet, but I've heard it's the best way –

NATASHA. *Mom.*

LYDIA. But whatever jet lag you have should wear off before too long; after all, you aren't leaving the country –

NATASHA. Mom, I'm *sorry.*

LYDIA. And you'll call when you land?

NATASHA. Yes. I already said that.

(*Offstage, the phone rings.*)

LYDIA. I'm expecting an important call. Be safe, darling.

(LYDIA *kisses* NATASHA, *and then exits.* MIKE *appears in the doorway.*)

MIKE. Ready to go?

NATASHA. Yes. *(beat)* I tried to tell her I –

MIKE. I know.

(MIKE *hugs* NATASHA.)

MIKE. Let's go.

(MIKE *and* NATASHA *exit.*)

Scene Nine

(A black vacuum onstage.)

LENA. We were a year older when we came back. I was seven and she was eight and a half, and it didn't occur to us then that the year away hadn't been a total waste. We had no way of knowing how much we'd miss the city, and our friends. And our mother, even though something about it felt sick and wrong. We didn't know how to appreciate it and we'd never even thought, before that year, of what it would be like not to have it. And for both of us, sitting in the back seat of the Volvo, looking out between the seats and over the dashboard as we drove across the bridge – it was like we'd never seen the city before. Not like that.

(Sound effect: the ding on an airplane.)

FLIGHT ATTENDANT'S VOICE. At this time, please turn off all electronic devices, including headsets and cell phones, and place your seats in the upright locked position as we prepare for take-off. A flight attendant will be moving through the cabin momentarily to ensure that all seatbelts are securely fastened.

(Lights up on the interior of an airplane. **LENA** *is mouthing the words and motioning along with the speech.* **NATASHA** *glances at her, then looks back at her, and shrieks.)*

LENA. Nice to see you, too.

*(**LENA** plops down next to **NATASHA**, who just stares at her.)*

LENA. Almost time for the video now. But you don't have to watch. No one does. Everybody just ignores it because if the plane really goes down –

NATASHA. I don't want to hear this.

LENA. It won't – but if it did, if you suddenly feel yourself plummeting towards earth –

(LENA opens up a small bag of peanuts and starts eating them.)

LENA. – If that happens, are you going to put on your oxygen mask and remain calm on the off chance you aren't a minute away from bursting into flames? Somehow, I don't think so –

NATASHA. What are you doing here?

LENA. Normally I'd say, "You look like you've seen a ghost," but in your case you look like you've never seen one before, which is just silly, so snap out of it. And quit looking at me all misty-eyed and contemplative, like something out of *Touched By An Angel*. You're making me uncomfortable. STOP it. What? You're not going to tell me you mind if I come along for the ride –

NATASHA. I don't know what's going on. I don't know what I'm doing here. I want peanuts.

LENA. You'll get yours. Once you've reached cruising altitude and the attendants can move freely about the cabin. Or they might be pretzels now, who knows? I told you to stop looking at me like that!

NATASHA. You disappear for months and then you magically decide to –

LENA. I was mad at you. I got over it. And plus, you know, you can't change your center of gravity. Even if she is completely lame –

NATASHA. I'm not completely lame.

(NATASHA reaches for her phone.)

LENA. No, he hasn't called you. You're supposed to turn that off because we're about to go.

(LENA takes the phone, shuts it off, and puts it back in the bag.)

CAPTAIN'S VOICE. Flight attendants, prepare for take-off.

LENA. Don't worry, Tasha, trust me. It's fun.

NATASHA. No, it isn't.

LENA. Did you see that one movie – that one with John Cusack and the radio and the end, the end is where the boy and the girl are on the plane –

NATASHA. Except I don't end up with John Cusack, do I?

LENA. I hope not. He's old. Now listen, at the end of the movie they're on the plane and they're waiting for the "ding" because –

NATASHA. I know, I know. I've seen it.

LENA. Does it make you feel better?

NATASHA. Not really.

(Pause; then, **NATASHA** *stands up.)*

It's going to crash –

LENA. It is *not*. Sit down.

*(***NATASHA*** obeys.)*

LENA. Let go of the armrests. Look out the window.

*(***NATASHA*** does; she's quiet for a moment. She takes a deep breath.)*

LENA. My sister Natasha can hold her breath for a long time. Long enough to scare people when we'd go to the lake or somebody's pool, enough to go through tunnels and past cemeteries. Not a world record – not long enough to cross the Golden Gate, but I know she still tries. I always thought that's funny, people who think it's a skill. That it will be good for something. Like one day, the bridge will decide it wants to collapse, and the only thing keeping it up and holding it all together, that giant, eight and a quarter mile mass of steel and concrete, is a little girl in the backseat of a family car. Face purple, holding her breath.

*(***LENA*** turns to look at her sister.)*

LENA. You can't hold it forever, Tasha.

*(***NATASHA*** grips the seat. She and* **LENA** *both look up, out, waiting. The bell dings in the cabin. Blackout.)*

End of Play

OTHER TITLES AVAILABLE FROM SAMUEL FRENCH

CROOKED

Catherine Trieschmann

Dramatic Comedy / 3f

Fourteen year old Laney arrives in Oxford, Mississippi with a twisted back, a mother in crisis and a burning desire to be writer. When she befriends Maribel Purdy, a fervent believer in the power of Jesus Christ to save her from the humiliations of high school, Laney embarks on a hilarious spiritual and sexual journey that challenges her mother's secular worldview and threatens to tear their fragile relationship apart.

"The work of a big accomplished writer's voice…a gem of a discovery."
- *The New York Times*

"Gorgeous almost beyond belief."
- *The Times, London*

"This is a wonderfully neat play, at once simple and complex, grappling with big issues - matters of faith, fantasy and the flesh - while keeping its sneakers firmly planted on the suburban topsoil of adolescent angst and domestic frictions."
- *The Daily Telegraph*

SAMUELFRENCH.COM

www.ingramcontent.com/pod-product-compliance
Lightning Source LLC
Chambersburg PA
CBHW070648300426
44111CB00013B/2329